SHADOWS WITH NO LIGHT

POETRY

BY

JASON CLAY ONEAL

© 2016 JASON CLAY ONEAL
ALL RIGHTS RESERVED

No part of this book may be reproduced or utilized in any form or by any means, electronic or mechanical, including information storage and retrieval system, without the prior written permission of the author or Spizzarri Entertainment Ltd.

Published by Spizzarri Entertainment Ltd.

PRINTED IN THE UNITED STATES OF AMERICA
THIS BOOK IS PRINTED ON ACID FREE PAPER

ISBN: 0-9779731-5-6

All poetry pieces,
cover art & photo:
Jason Clay Oneal

CONTACT ME ON TWITTER @JASONCONEAL
https://twitter.com/JASONCONEAL

CONTACT ME ON FACEBOOK AT:
https://www.facebook.com/SHADOWSWITHNOLIGHT

FOLLOW ME ON INSTAGRAM AT:
https://www.instagram.com/jason_c_oneal

EMAIL ME AT: SHADOWSWITHNOLIGHT@GMAIL.COM

THIS BOOK IS NOT DEDICATED TO ANYONE EXCEPT THOSE WHO HAVE FELT LIKE THEY NEVER BELONGED, THOSE THAT ALWAYS FELT ALONE IN ANY CROWDED ROOM AND THOSE THAT FEEL EVERYTHING SO MUCH THEY SUFFER.

THIS BOOK IS DEDICATED TO THE ONES WHO THINK OUTSIDE OF THE BOX OF "NORMALITY" INTELLECTS, QUEERS, HOMOSEXUALS, PUNKS, FREAKS, DYKES, FORWARD PROGRESSIVE OPEN MINDED THINKERS AND THE TRANS WORLD.

TO ANYONE THAT IS BRAVE ENOUGH TO ALWAYS BE WHO THEY TRULY ARE WITHOUT COMPROMISE AND WITHOUT WHO THEY ARE AROUND. THIS IS FOR THE REAL PEOPLE OUT THERE SO FEW AND FAR BETWEEN.

THIS BOOK IS FOR THE POOR AND THOSE THAT SPEND THEIR LIFE STRUGGLING JUST TO SURVIVE WITH POVERTY OR DEPRESSION AND MENTAL ILLNESS.

THIS IS FOR EVERYONE WHO DECIDED SUICIDE WAS THE BEST OPTION.

THIS BOOK IS A CULMINATION OF MANY YEARS OF FEELING TOO MUCH AND GETTING TOO LITTLE FROM A WORLD THAT IS NEVER ENOUGH.

THIS IS FOR RESTLESS SPIRITS WHO ARE NOT SATISFIED WITH SITTING IN FRONT OF A TELEVISION FOR HOURS EVERYDAY, WORKING AND GOING TO BED. THIS IS FOR THOSE THAT ARE TRULY AWARE AND AWAKE IN A WORLD OF DEAD ZOMBIES WALKING AROUND STARING INTO SCREENS OF SOME SORT ALL DAY.

THIS BOOK IS FOR PEOPLE WHO STILL PICK UP A PHYSICAL BOOK AND READ.

NOW MORE THAN EVER WE LIVE IN A WORLD WHERE REPRESSION IS KING, USE YOUR VOICE AND WORDS TO STAND UP AGAINST YOUR REPRESSORS.

IN THE PHYSICAL WORLD THIS BOOK IS DEDICATED TO THE RUGGED LIFETIME UNCONDITIONAL LOVE OF MY MOTHER AND TO THE 5 OR LESS SOULS THAT I WOULD REFER TO AS A TRUE FRIEND IN THIS LIFE.

A MASSIVE SHOW OF APPRECIATION FOR THOSE THAT DONATED TO THIS BOOK BEFORE IT WAS EVEN A REALITY.

A THANK YOU TO MUSIC, ART, FILM, BOOKS AND PHOTOGRAPHY FOR KEEPING ME ALIVE ON THIS MOSTLY DREADFUL PLANET.

REMEMBER LOVE AND HATE ARE EQUAL IF YOU BELIEVE IN THESE CONCEPTS.

LOVE YOURSELF FIRST, CONSIDER THE REST AND KEEP 10% ALWAYS TO YOURSELF.

ANGER IS A GIFT, LOVE ANIMALS AND SHOW LIVING THINGS THAT CANNOT DEFEND OR STAND UP FOR THEMSELVES PROTECTION AND COMPASSION IN THIS SAVAGE WORLD.

Generation dead, a bunch of passionless hard dicks with empty heads and hearts staring into phones blankly.

JASON CLAY ONEAL
11/8/2016

CONTENTS

1. 2 TWINS DIE
2. A LOVE LIKE THAT ENDS FASTER THAN A LOVE LIKE OURS
3. ANDROGYNOUS SHADOW
4. APPROACHING REFLECTIONS
5. ANTIQUE HEART
6. BAD RELIGION
7. BARE LIMBS
8. BREEDER LINGO
9. BI - POLAR SWING SET
10. BLACK ATHEIST
11. BLACK ICE
12. BLACK/WHITE
13. BLANKET COMA
14. BLOOD BIRD
16. BLOOD CLOT HEART
17. CORN FIELD CLOSET CROSS LOVE
18. CRACKS IN THE CEMENT
19. CRIPPLED RAYS OF MOTHER JESUS
20. DANCING FADING SHADOWS
21. DANGER OF HUMANS
22. DEATH GRIP
23. DEATHS WHISTLE
24. DIGITAL SLAVE
25. DIMINISHING WHITE LIGHT
26. DOPAMINE
27. EAR TO THE DOOR OF LIFE
28. FEELING
29. FLAMING BLOCK
30. FLESH LEGEND
32. FOG OF MAN
33. FROZEN FETUS
34. GENERATION NUMB
35. GHOSTS PASSING
36. HALF LIFE ABORTION
37. HALF SHADOW
38. HUMAN SHELL
39. INTENT VS REALITY
40. INTERSECTING DANGER

CONTENTS CONTINUED

- 41 IT'S THE NEWEST PHASE FOR CHAMELEON BOY
- 42 KISS
- 43 LETTER TO MY OTHER SELF
- 44 LIGHT LIKE STEPS ON A MOUNTAIN
- 46 LIGHT SWITCH EMOTION
- 47 LOATHING IN THE A.M.
- 48 LOVE THE CRACKED MIRROR
- 49 MASCULINE/FEMININE
- 50 MEMORY
- 51 MEMORY VOID
- 52 MISERY FUCK
- 53 MY DEATH
- 54 MY HEART IS BLANK (LIKE A PAGE IN THIS BOOK)
- 55 NAKED SORROW
- 56 NESTING
- 57 NO MATTER WHERE, THE BIRDS STILL SING THE SAME
- 58 NOTHING TO LIVE FOR AND YOU WOULD DIE FOR ANYTHING
- 60 OLD SOUL
- 61 OUTLOOK FADING
- 62 PAPER MISERY
- 63 PAPER WHORE
- 64 PERSONALITY DISTORTION
- 65 PLAYING THE UNIVERSE
- 66 PROMISE
- 67 RETURNING TO THE DREAM
- 68 ROLLING TIME
- 69 SAD DISTANCES
- 70 SEPARATION
- 71 SEXUAL DISORIENTATION
- 72 SHADOW FACE
- 73 SILENCE THE STARS
- 74 SKYWARD INNOCENCE
- 76 SPARK
- 77 SPIRIT DANCING - BODY IDLE
- 78 STACKED SOULS
- 79 STIFLED GROWTH
- 80 SYSTEMATIC CLOSET

CONTENTS CONTINUED

81 TEN PERCENT UNKNOWING
82 THE EYE OF WHIRLING EMOTION
83 THE ONLY DIFFERENCE BETWEEN ME
    AND THE PAVEMENT IS I FEEL
84 THE PAST IS UNFIXABLE
85 THE PEDAL DETERMINES
86 THE SIZE OF SMALL
87 THE SOIL CYCLES
88 THE TORNADO AND THE SNAKE
90 THOUGHT SEEPER
91 TIRED BRUISED BRAIN
92 TORMENTED BLISS
93 TOUGH BOY WITH THE PAINTED LIPS
94 UNDERSTANDING
95 WALKING MILES WITH THE BIBLE ON YOUR BACK
96 YOU CAN ONLY GO BACK IN YOUR HEAD

2 TWINS DIE

CRISS — CROSSED UMBIBLICAL CORD —
SHARE THIS BRAIN —
BLACK LIQUID DROWNING —
TRANSLUCENT SKIN —
SKELETAL STRUCTURE —
GRIPPING SMALL HANDS —
LET GO —
AS THE VACUMN SUCKS THE LIFE OUT OF US —
HEAR THE SCREAMS IN SILENCE —
ONE IN THE SAME —
CEREBRAL HEMORAGE —
ERASED OUR SHORT LIFE MEMORY —
NO HEAVEN —
NO HELL —
38 BREATHS —
AND THEN NOTHING —
THE SOIL CALLS US BACK —
THE EARTH CAN'T HANDLE —
BOTH OUR GHOSTS.

A LOVE LIKE THAT ENDS FASTER THAN A LOVE LIKE OURS

THE BEST THINGS TAKE TIME THEY SAY BUT PATIENCE
ALLUDES ME AND LEAVES MY HEART AT BAY—
HOLD ON FAST BECAUSE TIME IS FLYING BY.
IT KILLS ME INSIDE THE SOUND OF GOOD BYE.
WE HAVE ALL THE TIME IN THE WORLD YOU SAY
BUT URGENCY IS VITAL
RIGHT HERE TODAY.
IT IS SWALLOWING ME WHOLE AND DAYS
I AM DROWNING IN TEARS —
THE RESULT OF MY CONSTANT FEAR.
I TELL MYSELF EACH DAY THAT TIME IS MAKING US
STRONGER BUT DEEP INSIDE IT GETS HARDER.
I CAN IMAGINE MY LIFE WITHOUT YOU —
A YEARNING FOR MY TRUE FUTURE
DESIRES TO COME TRUE.
A LOVE LIKE THAT MAYBE IT WAS NOT TRUE —
THE ROMANCE ILLUSION THAT LIVES SECRETLY
IN MY HEAD AND HEART —
COLOR BLUE —
A FEELING NEW OR A PATTERN REPEATING —
A RHYTHM SO COMMON LIKE MOTHERS FETAL HEARTBEAT.

ANDROGYNOUS SHADOW

MORPHING — APPROACHING —
BRIMMING TO THE FLESH — BLOOD.
BARE LIKE A RAW EMOTION — UNCONFINED.
CHAOS —
DETERMINATION —
BRUISED —
THE BREAST OF HUMANITY REMOVED —
THE DARK BUSH OF YOUR SEXUALITY —
CAVE MAN — FEMINIST WOMAN —
THE FIST OF LOVE.
I COULD SMELL YOU APPROACHING.
DO NOT CONFUSE THESE DESIRES WITH
SOMETHING THAT MIGHT LAST.
IT WAS YOUR STOMACH THAT HELD
A THOUSAND ABORTED DREAMS.
WAS IT RAIN THAT ONCE FELL OR BLOOD?

APPROACHING REFLECTIONS

TOUCHING BARRIERS —
WE CAME TO THE SAME PLACE —
DRAWN LIKE A MIRROR.
HAND UP, TOUCHING FACE —
IS IT MINE?
EYES THAT SEE-SEE THINGS
THAT OTHERS DO NOT.
ONLY IN THIS MIRROR DO I SEE —
TOUCHING METALLIC HANDS THAT MELT —
FACES THAT DRIFT BUT WERE WHOLE
FOR A BRIEF MOMENT.
SPIRITS CROSSING THAT CONNECT.
FOR ONCE WE WERE NOT ALONE AND
ALIENS IN THIS WORLD.
LETTING IT GO BUT NOT LETTING YOU GO.
DID WE CROSS BUT ONCE OR WILL WE CROSS AGAIN?
THE EVERLASTING HAZE ABOVE OUR HEADS
DO YOU CALL THIS MEMORY?

ANTIQUE HEART

FRAMED FOR THE AGES
YOU LOOKED DOWN IN SORROW
PICTURE CAPTURED MOMENT
5 CORNERS OF MY MIND
CHAINED ANKLES — BURIED
SECRETS — OLD HEART — MR. SAD
LITTLE MAN ALWAYS LOOKING UP AT ME
LIKE MARCHING AUTHORITY.
PLANTED SEED THAT NEVER GREW
VINTAGE TIME — BLIND GENERATIONS
THE MARCHING SOLIDER
NUMB TO STINGING SNOW — MOTIONLESS
STARE FRAMED EXISTENCE
MECHANICAL INSIDES
BLACK KISS
WALK INTO THE MIRROR —
TO GET TO THE OTHER SIDE.

BAD RELIGION

YOUR HISTORY — A LIE —
DID YOU EVER QUESTION — THE COMFORT OF A LIE —
LIVING IN A SPACE UNCHANGED.
ONE THOUSAND YEARS —
40 HOURS — STOLEN TIME —
YOU BELIEVE IT — NOT ME —
THE RELIGION IT BLEEDS — IT BLINDS —
IT CAUSED THIS WAR INSIDE —
INTERNAL HATE —
LIFE — LONG BATTLE —
YOU WILL NEVER WIN — BUT IN YOUR HEAD YOU HAVE.
A DATE WITH REALITY — BUT YOU KEPT CANCELLING —
THE STORM — RAINING CONFLICT —
ADDICTED — THIS FEELING —
IT IS IN THE MIDDLE OF THIS TORNADO
THAT I FINALLY FOUND PEACE.
TIME —
THE ENEMY TO MY BAD RELIGION.

BARE LIMBS

THE BARE LIMBS OF THE TREE —
WAITING TO ABSORB MEMORIES —
SOLID —
STILL —
FULL OF POTENTIAL LIFE — APPEARING DEAD.
EYE DECEIVING —
I SEE SO MUCH — YOU FEEL NOSTALGIC —
YOU FEEL LIKE A BETTER TIME —
FEELINGS —
DEPROGRAMMED —
DESOLATE —
SNOW WAITING —
WINTER SOLACE — COLORS UNSEEN —
FUTURE LOVERS NEVER THERE BUT IN MIND —
COMFORT —
TIME STAND STILL —
SPINNING BUT I COULDN'T FEEL —
YOU WOULD NEVER GUESS.

BREEDER LINGO

BABY FACTORY —
LINED UP —
FETUS DEPT —
BRO —
DUDE —
MAN —
THE GRIP OF A BEER IN ONE HAND —
BABY IN ANOTHER —
HE COMES TO ME WHEN HE LEAVES YOU —
INNOCENT FEMALE —
STOLEN IDENITY —
SPORTS MONSTER —
GROWL —
CHEST BEATING CUM FILLED SIMPLETON —
YOU LEFT THE SCAR ON ME —
SHOOT IN ME —
YOU CANNOT LOVE US BOTH —
BUT IM ADDICTED TO OUR HALF LIFE NOTION —
THE IDEA OF LOVE AND DANGER.

BI — POLAR SWING SET

EMOTIONS REVERTING —
CONFUSION —
TO THE FRONT —
TO THE BACK —
TEARS CRAWLING UP THE MOUNTAIN —
NEVER REACHING THE TOP —
BACKWARDS THINKING —
HIGH —
TOO HIGH —
LOW —
LIKE THE THOUSAND YEAR OLD RIVER NOW
PART OF THE LANDSCAPE OF MY MIND —
DRY NOW —
NO MORE DROWNING EMOTIONS —
VOID MY NEW HOME —
LOVE EVICTION —
DON'T COME HERE ANYMORE —
WHEELCHAIR SITTING IN THE
SAME PLACE FOR YEARS —
PUSHED TOO FAR AND NOW I HAVE FALLEN OFF.

BLACK ATHEIST

CHOKING ON THE GIFT OF OXYGEN —
THE VIEW YOU HAVE NARROWED SO SMALL —
NO ONE CAN FIT —
DREAMS SO VIBRANT —
IT IS THERE WE ARE ALIVE —
WHEN I WAKE I HAVE REALLY DIED —
THE ROUGH HANDS OF ANCIENT WOMEN —
BURNING SUN ROBBED YOU OF YOUR YOUTH —
IN THE WHEEL OF LIFE —
HAPPINESS WAS NEVER AN OPTION —
FIELDS AND LULLABIES —
SAILORS FROM IMAGINARY SHIPS —
BAREFOOT —
DRAGGING ALONG THE SHORES OF OCEANS UNKNOWN.

BLACK ICE

BLACK GLARE —
HIDDEN FATALITIES —
NO CONTROL —
MILES OF RISK —
DARK NIGHT — DANGER —
ASPHALT KISS —
ON 2 KNEES —
MOON GUIDING US TO A PREDETERMINED FATE —
A NOD OFF —
DISCONNECT —
THE LIFE SUPPORT —
A HIDDEN FORCE —
CLOUDS AND SUN DO NOT MATTER NOW —
SLIDING INTO TRAGEDY —
FALLING OFF A MOUNTAIN OR SLIPPING INTO FOREVER.

BLACK/WHITE

SUN/MOON
DAY/NIGHT
START/FINISH
DARK/LIGHT
WIN/FAIL
TIME STANDS STILL — (INTERLUDE)
FAST/SLOW
HARD/SOFT
HOLD ME — HIT ME
SCAR — SKIN — HEALED WOUNDS.

BLANKET COMA

SMOTHERED IN THE DRAKNESS OF SECURITY —
THE HEAT FROM YOUR BREATH —
BLOCKED THE OUTSIDE WORLD —
THE SIGNS OF LIFE — BEYOND THE WINDOWS —
OR THE PRISON —
STORMED ANXIETY — EMPTY MOUTH —
FED WITH PACIFYING INVISIBLE KISSES OF MY UGLY SIDE —
IT IS JUST THE TWO OF US NOW —
CLOSED EYES BRING MOVIE LIKE DREAMS —
BEATING HEARTS THAT WOKE US.

BLOOD BIRD

BLOOD BIRD — PECKING HUMANITY
DRONE WITH A HEARTBEAT
WATCHING FROM ABOVE — VIEW
LAUGHING WITH A RAGE
DEMENTED SCAVENGER
FREE BUT AT WHAT COST?
COVERED IN THE BLOOD OF MANY —
THE MIND OF A FEW
BLOOD WITH A TASTE OF SALT —
LIKE THE TIME MY WOUNDS BURNED
KEEP POURING IT IN NOW
I AM NUMB
BRAIN EATER —
SUCKING THE NIPPLES OF HUMANITY DRY
GIVE ME MORE —
THERE IS NEVER ENOUGH —
THERE NEVER WILL BE
LACKING CONTENT —
THE BLOOD DRIPS FROM MY EYE —
MISTAKEN FOR A TEAR.

BLOOD CLOT HEART

FROZEN — HISTORY — STOP
A DREAM WHERE I OBSERVE BUT DO NOT TAKE PART —
OUTSIDE —
A WAVE THAT NEVER REACHES ANY SHORE —
THAT HAS NOW BECOME A TSUNAMI OF THOUGHTS.
WE CHANGE CLOTHES BUT WE NEVER
CAN CHANGE THE HEART BENEATH —
I COUNTED ONCE THE TIMES YOU BEAT IN A MINUTE —
THEN I LOST THE WILL TO KEEP COUNTING.
BLOOD CLOT HEART —
BREATHING —
THE STOP SIGN REMINDED TO STOP LOVING —
TO STOP NEEDING ME —
TO STOP SEEKING.
BLOOD CLOT HEART —
YOU STOPPED IT FROM HAPPENING AGAIN — FOR NOW.
IT SEEMED SO GOOD —
BUT NOTHING IS EVER WHAT IT SEEMS —
IS IT?

CORN FIELD CLOSET CROSS LOVE

YOU SAID YOUR HEART WAS NO LONGER IN IT —
TIME INVESTED CANNOT BE TAKEN BACK —
SO MUCH —
MORE THAN ANYONE —
I AM SICK WITH THE KNOWLEDGE OF WHAT WE SHARED —
COULD BE INVADED BY ANOTHER FLESH WHORE —
EMOTIONS SO HIGH —
AND SO LOW.

CRACKS IN THE CEMENT

I LOOKED IN THE REFLECTION OF
YOUR WORDS THAT BURN —
I COULDN'T SEE BEHIND THEM —
DID THEY HAVE A BACKBONE —
FEAR LIKE FORCE — FED FECES —
IN TIME YOU WILL GROW TO LIKE ANYTHING —
THE MIND PROTECTS ITSELF —
ISN'T IT FUNNY HOW THINGS WORK —
PASSION IS NON-EXISTENT IN THIS DIGITAL AGE —
THE AVENUES THAT THE GHOST
OF ROMANCE WALKS ENDLESSLY —
IF I HAD ONLY TURNED THAT CORNER.

CRIPPLED RAYS OF MOTHER JESUS

ALTAR — WEAK WOMEN — SLAVE TO MAN'S CHURCH —
MADE BY MAN FOR A MAN WITH A MAN'S THOUGHTS.
SLAVE WITH THE GOLDEN OYSTER —
SHE IS MISSING IN YOUR STORY —
AFTER THE SNAKE RAVAGES HER — SHE RISES UP
ILLUMINATED BY A BURNING CANDLE —
NO LIFE LEFT —
BUT ENOUGH TO KEEP HOLDING ON —
TAKE A SWORD TO THIS MAN WHO TRAPS THE MIND —
BLOOD DROPS FROM THE STRUGGLE
AS SHE RIDES THE WHITE HORSE
INTO THE KINGDOM —
HER HEAD WRAPPED —
SHE COLLAPSED AND WAS DRAGGED AWAY
LIKE SO MANY BEFORE HER —
INTO THE ABYSS OF A MAN'S STORY.

DANCING FADING SHADOWS

WHIRLING SPIRITS OF LONG GONE FLESH —
WE LEFT THE RESTRAINTS OF GRAVITY
TO FREE OUR BODIES OF THE BURDENS IT BRINGS.
WE ADDED COLOR TO THIS BLACK AND WHITE EXISTENCE.
WE DIED AND HEAVEN NEVER CAME BUT
WE ESCAPED THE HELL OF FLESH.
EACH DOT FILLING IN YOUR FACE — NEVER COMPLETE —
LIKE A HALF MOON —
THE SHADOW OF YOUR GRAVE —
EMPTY.
I CANNOT PAY THE PRICE FOR YOUR STOLEN PASSIONS.
DANGLING MAN HOOD —
THE SMELL OF YOU —
THE PART OF YOU THAT WILL NEVER DRIP OUT OF ME.
I ALWAYS SEE YOUR SHADOW IN THE DISTANCE
WHEN MY EYES ARE CLOSED.
IN MY SLEEP I FEEL ALIVE —
IT IS WHEN I OPEN THEM I AM DEAD.

DANGER OF HUMANS

PROWLING —
FOOT CREEPING —
TINTED WINDOWS —
WITH LIFE'S GANGSTER —
THE LEFT BEHIND —
NO ONE LOVES YOU —
GHETTO DWELLER —
THE GOVERNMENT LOVER —
CONTROL —
THE DIGITAL LEASH YOU ARE KEPT ON —
I KEPT WALKING DOWN STAIRS THAT NEVER ENDED —
IT IS DARK NOW —
HEART RACING —
WALK FASTER —
THE DANGER OF THE UNKNOWN —
IT IS A SHAME YOU HAVE TO TRUST HUMANS —
WAS THERE A STEP MISSING ON YOUR WAY DOWN.

DEATH GRIP

TREE HUGGING —
THE ANCIENT VINTAGE STORIES IT HIDES —
SQUEEZING —
AS IF TO SAY —
FOR ONCE I HAVE WHAT I ALWAYS WANTED —
DARK CLOUD DANGER —
EMBRACE WHAT IS LEFT OF
YOUR FORGOTTEN LIFE —
ASH —
BONE —
STONE —
100 YEARS —
ROOTS —
DEEPER THAN THE FAILING ARTERIES
OF THE BLACK HEART —
SYMPHONY OF THE BLACK BIRD CRYING —
SOILED HAND REACHING UP —
I CANNOT BREATHE SHE SAID —
CAN YOU DIG UP MY CHILDREN —
AND MAKE SURE THEY ARE OK.

DEATHS WHISTLE

DEATHS WHISTLE LIKE THE NIGHT TRAIN
HEARD IN THE DISTANCE —
EACH WHEEL TURNING LIKE A PASSING BODY
TO NOTHINGNESS —
END RESULT —
DUST —
YOUR NEW HOME A BOX —
EVEN THEN DO WE FIND PEACE —
LEAVING FLESH BURDENS AND FAILED ORGANS —
DO WE STILL FEEL TOO MUCH HERE —
I TRAVEL MORE SINCE I HAVE DIED —
WITHOUT ACTUALLY MOVING —
DID YOU HEAR THAT SOUND OR IS IT JUST MY TURN?

DIGITAL SLAVE

TECHNOLOGY IS YOUR DISTRACTION
CLICK — CLACK
KEYBOARD TOUCH REPLACED THE HUMAN TOUCH
STARE INTO THE SCREEN
THE ONLY LIGHT OF THE APPLE
YOU LOST THE ABILITY TO INTERACT
BEYOND A BLANK SCREEN
WHICH REPLACED THE BLANK STARE OF A HUMAN —
BORING NOW —
UNINSPIRED —
THE ONLY PASSION COMES FROM A BRIEF CYBER RANT
SEEN BY FEW AND SCROLLED PAST UNNOTICED
BY HUNDREDS — CALLED A NEWSFEED —
LEAVING YOU HUNGRY FOR MORE
DO YOU ABSORB THOUGH —
OR JUST SEE?
FORCE FED —
A GLUTEN FREE VERSION OF WHAT YOU MIGHT CALL
A PERSONALITY —
ABSENT.

DIMINISHING WHITE LIGHT

CRYING —
PLEADING MID-WINTER TEARS —
FROZEN IN PLACE —
LIKE THE LIFE OF THE SEX WORKER —
BLOOD CLOT KISSES AND TWENTY DOLLAR
MOMENTS OF HOPE —
EMPTY BOTTLES —
RATTLING PILLS —
STOLEN MASCARA —
GOODWILL DRESS —
BLANK EYES —
TORN FISHNETS —
LIKE THE CHILDHOOD TORN FROM HER —
THE ONLY WARMTH NOW FOUND IN HER HEART —
COMES FROM THE TANNING BED AND
TOUCH OF HER WRINKLED SKIN.

DOPAMINE

DRIED —
HANGING ON BY STRANDS OF THREAD —
BUILT IN —
NOT WANTING TO DIE —
NOT WANTING TO LIVE —
CRAWLING —
I CRAWLED TO YOU —
WRITTEN WORD —
UNSPOKEN THOUGHT —
REPETITION —
LIFE —
ANXIETY —
IF THERE IS ONE THING THAT WILL
ALWAYS BE THERE —
IT IS YOU —
GENDERLESS —
NO HUMAN IN YOUR —
HUMAN NATURE.

EAR TO THE DOOR OF LIFE

SWEAT REMINDS ME —
I AM AMONGST THE SHRILL LIVING —
HEART BEAT RACING AS I HEAR THE
SMAL MINDED FAMILIES AROUND ME —
A HEART THAT LIVED THROUGH SO MANY WARS —
BUT KEEPS FIGHTING —
MY MIND IS THE MASTER —
AND I THE SLAVE TO IT'S DEMANDS —
SITTING INSIDE MY HEAD LIKE A PILOT TO THE PLANE —
YOU CONTROL ME —
I BEAT MY HEAD HARDER BUT YOU NEVER GO AWAY —
IF I HOLD MY BREATH LONG ENOUGH —
WILL THIS ANXIETY HEART STOP BEATING.

FEELING

SHUT YOU OFF —
LIKE A LIGHT SWITCH —
I WISH IT WAS SO EASY —
YOU NEVER ACTUALLY HIT ME WITH YOUR FIST —
BUT YOUR WORDS OR LACK OF
HIT HARDER THAN YOUR FIST EVER COULD.

FLAMING BLOCK

EYES COVERED —
PROTECTION — MOTHER AFRICA —
FLAMING BRAIN — THOUGHTS ON FIRE.
CORPSE ON FIRE —
SHELTERED — NURTURED —
THE FEAR FOR BOTH OF US IN HER EYES.
RESTRAINT — SO CLOSE —
BLOCKED.
SHE KNOWS WHAT YOU JUST ASSUMED.
SHE IS AWARE IN PLACES YOU ARE ASLEEP —
THESE TWO.
IS THAT FIRE OR THE SUN REFLECTING
MY DESIRES ONTO YOUR FACE?
IF YOU TURN YIUR HEAD YOU WILL SEE TOO —
BUT MOST CHOOSE TO STAY BLIND.

FLESH LEGEND

RAMPAGE OF AGING FLESH —
SO SIMPLE —
SO LEGENDARY TO SOME —
A CLASSIC FLESH ORGAN PENETRATED BY SO MANY —
FLESH LEGENDS —
THE LASTING SAGA OF A PAPER NOTE —
NOT EARNED BY ANYTHING MORE THAN WHOREDOM —
PLASTIC LIKE A DOLL —
MAKE UP COVERS WRINKLES TOO DEEP TO FIX —
INJECT ME WITH THE YOUTHFUL NEEDLE —
BUT THE OLD HEART CAN'T BE FIXED OR UPDATED —
IT IS OLD LIKE THE BLOOD THAT FLOWS —
THROUGH YOUR EMPTY VEINS.

FOG OF MAN

THERE IS NO FUTURE, BUT YOU WOULD NEVER GUESS
FROM EACH FAST PASSING DAY —
PILED UP WITH THE DAWN AND DUSK.
SQUIRTING SEED OF MAN.
MOUTH WATERING SOUR INDUCING VOMIT —
15 MINUTES
AND THE IDEA MAKES ME ILL.
ORGAN - THE CENTER OF OUR EXISTENCE.
SO MUCH EMPHASIS ON THE HUNT —
THE HUNT THAT LEAVES YOU WITH A 3 LETTER WORD.
THE END RESULT IS A PART TAKEN
THAT YOU CAN NEVER GET BACK.
IS ALL THIS GIVING AWAY WORTH THE
TEMPORARY HOLDING ON?
HANDS ALWAYS OPEN, GRABBING ONTO
FLESH AS IF YOU WERE HOLDING ONTO FOG.
THESE THINGS YOU CANNOT HOLD ON TO.

FROZEN FETUS

BRIDGING HUMANITY — FROZEN LIFE —
NO FLOWING BLOOD —
ICED HEART WITH CLEAR VISION —
I STARTED OFF SEEING SO CLEAR —
SEE THRU — ONE EYE COVERED —
OFF IN THE DISTANCE.
FROZEN MEMORY —
ALONE WITH YOURSELF —
TORMENTED —
FROZEN RIVER — I JUMPED IN BUT MY ARMS
WILL NOT LET ME SWIM —
AM I DROWNING?
I ASKED MY DYING SELF.
SWIM TOWARD THE BLUE LIGHT OF IMAGINATION —
HIS MOUTH MOVED TO ANSWER — BUT HE SLIPPED AWAY.
I OPENED MY MOUTH BUT NO WATER RUSHED IN.
I WAS FLOATING IN THE FINAL MOMENTS —
BEFORE MY REBIRTH.
THAW THIS HEART —
SO I CAN REMEMBER WHAT RED LOOKS LIKE.

GENERATION NUMB

PLUGGED IN BUT NEVER TUNED IN —
STARE INTO THE BLANK SCREEN —
SMILES IN DARK ROOMS —
NO ONE EVER ENTERS —
BESIDES MILENIAL NUMBNESS —
DOCTOR SO EAGER TO WRITE THE PRESCRIPTION —
BUT NO PILL EXISTS FOR THIS LONELINESS —
YOUR LIFE LOVE IS YOUR DEVICE —
FACE TO FACE —
A MEMORY OF BETTER TIMES —
THE DIGITAL AGE —
THE ROBOT NAMED EMOTION —
REPROGRAMMED TO FEEL NOTHING IN THE YEAR 0000.

GHOSTS PASSING

HIGHWAYS INTERSECTING —
SPIRITS —
THOUGHT PATTERNS —
GHOSTS PASSING THROUGH US —
SIDEWALK FULL OF HUMAN RATS —
RACING TO THE NEXT DREAM —
I FEEL YOU IN THE GUSTS OF WIND —
YOU BLEW ME INTO THE OCEAN —
AND I DROWNED IN YOUR LIQUID MEMORY —
THE STORIES TOLD BY MOVING LIPS —
POWERED BY NO BEATING HEART —
THESE STREETS FULL OF THE LIVING DEAD —
WHO WAS PLASTIC —
AND WHO WAS FLESH.

HALF LIFE ABORTION

WE FELL IN LIFE'S SINK HOLE —
SLID TO THE BOTTOM —
BUT CRAWLING ON THE EDGES —
THAT CRACK OF LIGHT SO SMALL —
NEVER GUIDING US TO ESCAPE —
CRUELTY THAT ALLOWS US THIS
EMPTY THING CALLED HOPE —
GREAT WAY TO FOOL ME —
BRAIN SO BIG —
HEART SO SMALL —
TELL ME ANOTHER FAIRY TALE —
SUCK ME IN AND MAYBE THEN —
THIS ARTIFICIAL HEART CAN BEAT AGAIN —
STOP ME HALFWAY.

HALF SHADOW

IS THERE ENOUGH BLOOD TO KEEP
BOTH OUR HEARTS BEATING —
IN THIS NEW VERSION YOU CALL LIFE?
THIS OVER-TIRED EARTH —
SPINNING SOMEHOW —
EACH HUMAN —
NOTHING BUT HER BURDEN —
YOUR ONLY CONTRIBUTION —
A BEER BOTTLE IN A LANDFILL —
AS THE SHADOW OF HER SUN —
COVERED THE FACES OF SHAME —
DID THE BLOOD CLOT BLOCK YOUR CONSCIENCE?
MOTHER EARTH IN A SHORT DRESS —
DO YOU THINK SHE'S A WHORE?
DID YOU PENETRATE HIM WITH KNOWLEDGE —
OR KILL HIS ABILITY TO THINK —
BY TURNING ON THE TV?

HUMAN SHELL

LAYERED PROTECTION —
TO THE BONE —
SPIRIT SHELL —
UNDER ARMOR SKELETAL —
THAT'S ALL WE LEAVE WITH —
CANCER CANNOT PENETRATE —
CANCER CANNOT DESTROY —
THIS ONE THING —
FLESH TONE —
BEAUTIFUL —
COVERING UP ALL THE UGLY ORGANS UNDERNEATH —
FORCE UNCONTROLLED —
YOU CALL NATURE —
THE BEAST —
YOUR MONEY CANNOT FIX THIS NATURAL DEVIL —
WHO DECIDES FOR YOU —
HELPLESS —
BUILT WITH NO CONSCIENCE —
THESE THINGS —
THAT REQUIRE A BEATING HUMAN HEART.

INTENT VS REALITY

DIMMING HORIZON —
DETOURS OF LIFE —
CIRCLES —
MEMORIES LAND ON THE BRAIN LIKE SNOW FLAKES
MELT WITH THE HEAT.
CAPACITY —DEPTH —INTENT —
PEEL BACK THE LAYERS —
IT'S STILL NOT THERE —
DARK ROADS TRAVELED DO NOT
REVEAL THE SECRETS OF MISTRESS SUNLIGHT.
TRACK MARKS —
MOTHER'S NEEDLE IS ALMOST EMPTY.
THE THOUGHT IS NEVER AS GOOD AS THE REALITY.

INTERSECTING DANGER

EACH CHANCE TAKEN —
TENSION —
THE WHAT IF…
I STALLED IN THE INTERSECTION OF LIFE —
A CHANCE TO CRASH WITH ALL THE
INTERCHANGABLE LIVES —
COMING AT ME —
HEAD DOWN —
NO EYE CONTACT —
I CONNECT THEN DISCONNECT —
CHANCES FOR RESOLUTION —
A HEART WITH ADHD —
A BRAIN STUCK IN A RECURRING
BLACK AND WHITE MEMORY —
30 SECONDS TO DANGER —
WE SURVIVED ANOTHER DAY —
A LUNG SCREAMING AND GASPING
FOR ONE MORE BREATH —
OUR PERSONALITIES COLLIDING —
LIKE A CAR ON A WINDING COUNTRY ROAD AT 3AM —
WITH NO HEADLIGHTS —
DID YOU SENSE THE INTERSECTING DANGER?
THE POSSIBILITIES ARE ENDLESS —
IF ONLY IT WASN'T THE END.

IT'S THE NEWEST PHASE FOR CHAMELEON BOY

COAT CHANGING WITH SEASONS —
PEEL OFF THE LAYERS —
IS THERE A TRUE PERSON THERE —
DROWN ME IN THE WATERS AND I WILL COME BACK —
THE MIRROR IS YOUR ENEMY —
DO YOU SEE YOURSELF IN EVERYONE ELSE —
THE BLINDS WERE CLOSED —
THE SKIN WAS BARE —
THE PILLOW SILENCED YOUR SELF HATING SCREAMS —
HOW MANY PHASES BEFORE —
THE MIRROR CRACKS AFTER YOU
STARE IN IT LONG ENOUGH —
TO SEE YOUR TRUE REFLECTION.

KISS

KISS SO INTIMATE —
YOU WENT TO SPEAK BUT I ATE YOUR WORDS —
YOU PLANTED THE SEED IN ME —
YOU STOLE SO MANY PARTS OF ME —
I CAN'T GET BACK.
I SWALLOWED SO MANY OF YOUR WORDS —
AND NOW WHEN I SPEAK IT IS FOR YOU.

LETTER TO MY OTHER SELF

DEAREST JASON —
I AM YOUR HEAVY HEART —
I WEIGH YOU DOWN EVERYDAY —
SINCE THAT SELFISH MAN WITH THE
NEXT BEST THING SYNDROME —
LEFT YOU TO BLEED —
LIKE A DEER ON A DARK 2 LANE ROAD —
SLOWLY DYING —
ALMOST EMPTY —
IT WAS A 2 WAY STREET —
BUT YOU'RE THE ONE GOING IN CIRCLES —
NEVER REACHING A DESTINATION —
HE ARRIVED WE GUESS —
WITH NO THOUGHT OF YOU.

LIGHT LIKE STEPS ON A MOUNTAIN

I ONLY SEEN YOU FROM A DISTANCE SO OFTEN —
THE TIME CAME —
I EXITED AND STARED YOU DOWN TO LOOK BACK
AT MELTING ASPHALT IN THE GLARING LIGHT
YOU CALL SUN —
ALL THOSE STEPS AHEAD —
AND ALL THAT ROAD BEHIND —
HAVE I REALLY BEEN STANDING STILL THIS WHOLE TIME —
EACH STEP INVITING LIKE ALL THE MONTHS
OF MY PASSING LIFE —
FOR ONCE YOU WHISPERED —
YOU CANNOT GO BACK.

LIGHT SWITCH EMOTION

ON — OFF — LIGHT — DARK —
EMPTY ROOM — EMPTY HEART —
FULL STOMACH — I PURGED YOU FROM THE DEEPEST
PARTS OF MY BEING BUT YOUR SCAR IS TOO DEEP
THERE IS NO BOTTOM AND NO END TO THE LURKING
SHADOW THAT ALWAYS FOLLOWS
WHEN I GET LOST YOU ALWAYS FIND THE WAY TO ME
NO INBETWEEN
LIKE A LANE THAT NARROWS I AM FORCED TO CRASH
INTO YOU BUT I GO RIGHT THROUGH YOU.
THE ROOTS PLANTED IN ME
SEEDS OF SORROW
DEAD ROOTS
TICKING CLOCK
TURN ME ON — TURN ME OFF
CEASE TO BREATH.

LOATHING IN THE A.M.

SUN SICK —
SHADOW INDUCING NAUSEA —
THIS DESPERATE HOUR —
THE HAPPY PEOPLE IN THE CORPORATE BUILDINGS —
STARING THROUGH THE WINDOWS —
DOWN UPON YOU AND ME —
BLIND REFLECTIONS —
AMNESIA COMFORTS ME —
IF I REMEMBERED I WOULD BE NUMB —
THE COCOON WRAPPING ME WITH THIS PEACE —
AS THE RAT RACE HUMMING CRASHES THE SILENCE —
5AM TO NOON —
TIME LIKE THE STRANGLER OF THE MORNING MEMORY —
LET GO —
BEFORE I DIE.

LOVE THE CRACKED MIRROR

I LOVE THE CRACKED MIRROR —
IT IS THERE I CAN FINALLY SEE —
ALL MY PERSONALITIES.

MASCULINE/FEMININE

THE SPARK INSIDE —
HIS BURNING MAN — HOOD —
HUNGRY TO SPREAD THE MASCULINE
CHOKE HOLD ON THIS FEMININE BEING —
SUBMISSION SO INTENSE —
BEGGING TO FEEL HUMILIATION —
STAMP ME WITH YOUR GENDER BEING —
HE SAID —
IN THE VOICE OF A HELIUM BITCH —
THE WASPS STING NEVER HURTS AS GOOD AS THIS —
WORKING MAN —
SISSY BOY —
SECRETS BEHIND 100 YEAR OLD DOORS —
OPEN ME UP WIDER THAN MOUTHS OF SINNERS —
GAGGING ON THE LIQUID —
OF MAN'S SEED.

MEMORY

YOU CREATE NOSTALGIA —
EVERY TIME I DRIVE DOWN YOUR HIGHWAYS —
I LONG FOR THE LAST TIME —
WILL THERE BE A NEXT TIME?

MEMORY VOID

BLANK SPACES —
LIKE BLANK STARES —
MEMORY NEVER VOIDED —
CREEPING INTO MY DAYS —
CASTING LIVABLE SHADOWS
WHERE ONE NEVER REALLY WAS —
I CAN'T REMOVE THIS-STAIN ETERNAL LIKE A SCAR —
REMINDERS —
DECADES AND LAYERS —
NAKED BRAIN —
BARE TO HURT BY YOUR CONSTANT
INVASIONS OF PRESUMED SAFE ZONES —
ONE DAY LIKE THIS WALKING AND BREATHING CORPSE —
YOU WILL BE NOTHING BUT BONE AND ASH.

MISERY FUCK

MISERY —
YOU FUCKED ME HARDER THAN ANY
MAN'S THROBBING FLESH COULD
BUT UNLIKE THE HUMAN FLAW OF ABANDONMENT —
YOU NEVER LEFT.
LIKE A SHADOW IN THE CORNER OF MY EYE —
BUT YOU WERE NOT AN ILLUSION —
THE ONLY ILLUSION LIVED IN MY CREATION OF YOU —
I CREATED THE IMAGE —
I WAS IN LOVE WITH LOVE.
I PUT YOU TO SLEEP AND NO ONE
TRIED OR CARED TO WAKE YOU.
LIFE SUPPORT —
IS THIS LIFE?
DEFINE ME —
YEARS —
I SUCKED THE UTTERS OF YOUR MILK —
BUT YOUR SEED NEVER IMPREGNATED ME
WITH ANYTHING —
BUT CONSTANT SORROW.

MY DEATH

MY DEATH LAYING NEXT TO ME —
BREATHING IN UNISON WITH MY SPIRIT —
ABRUPTLY AWOKEN FROM THE OTHER LIFE I KNOW —
2 DREAMS RUNNING —
BLACK AND WHITE —
WITH NO GRAY —
MY CONSTANT COMPANION —
WOULD EMOTION BE JEALOUS —
IF HE KNEW OF THIS AFFAIR —
OF THE IMAGINATION —
THE HALO —
A SIGN OF OUR CEREMONY —
THE SOIL MUST BE SO COMFORTING —
NOW IT IS MY ETERNAL COMPANION —
I BEGAN TO ASK —
BUT MY MIND COULD NOT GET THESE
COLD PALE LIPS TO MOVE —
LIKE THE SUN I WILL NEVER SEE AGAIN.

MY HEART IS BLANK
(LIKE A PAGE IN THIS BOOK)

PERCEPTION IS WHAT KILLS ME.
THE LACK OF ATTENTION.
DAYS I SPEND WALKING IN A DREAM BECAUSE
THE REALITY IS EMOTIONALLY OVERWHELMING.
LOVE CAME WITHOUT ANY NOTICE AND THEN
A PART OF ME THAT WAS FROZEN AND BITTER WAS
THAWED TO A POINT OF LIQUID LIKE THE TEARS
THAT POUR FROM MY EYES AT TIMES.
THE ROAD SO OPEN AND WIDE.
THE SPACE BETWEEN US AS I MOVE FURTHER AWAY.
MY HEART BLANK (LIKE THE MORNING SUNS GLARE)
FALLING IN LOVE IS LIKE DRIVING HEAD ON
INTO THE GLARING MORNING SUN.
THE ROAD THOUGH NEVERENDING —
GIVES THE ILLUSION THAT YOUR GETTING
CLOSER TO YOUR DESTINATION.
A DESTINATION THAT IS NOT A REALITY
BUT A BLINDING HOPE —
A BLINDING FAITH THAT JUST LIKE
THE SUN YOU WILL NEVER GET TO.
TAKE ME IN YOUR ARMS LIKE A
LUNG COVERED IN SMALL HOLES —
THAT'S HOW I LOOK AT MY HEART.
SO MANY SMALL HOLES —
SO MANY DISAPPOINTMENTS THAT LEAD UP
TO THIS HOLE NOW LARGER THAN LIFE.
A BLACK HOLE OF FAILURE AND HURT —
NEVER — ENDING PAIN LIKE THAT
ROAD THAT NEVER ENDS.
THE MILES ON MY HEART SO
VAST AND BROKE DOWN —
IT IS A WONDER THIS HEART STILL BEATS.

NAKED SORROW

THE FORREST OF THOUGHT —
THE PLACE I AM NAKED EVEN WITH
FABRIC COVERING THE DARK PARTS
OF MY MIND —
THE TREE — EACH LIMB A CRACK IN THE HEART —
LIMBS OF TIME SEEING SO MUCH
BUT ONLY THE BIRD KNOWS WHEN TO
REALLY FLY AND CUT THIS ONE STRING
THAT TRAPS YOU TO THIS MEMORY
CUP OF SORROW — LINED UP —
WE TAKE AIM NEVER HITTING.
WAS IT BAD AIM OR WERE WE
ALWAYS SET UP TO FAIL?
WE WISH WE COULD THINK
OUR WAY OUT OF THIS —
THE URGE IS ALWAYS THERE
BECAUSE A BLACK EYE WILL
ALWAYS HEAL AND FADE BUT —
THE SCAR OF LOVE IS ETERNAL.

NESTING

FATHER OF MY WORLD — WHERE ARE YOU
AFTER THE NATURAL INSTINCT PUMPS
THE SEED IN ME — WHO IS LOST —
A SIMPLE REASON TO BE.
MOTHER OF THE WORLD — BACKBONE —
IT NEVER TAKES A MAN TO BARE YOUR PAIN .
THOSE FIRST 5 YEARS —
THE WIPED UP TEARS OF YOUR BABY BOY —
NEVER WANTING TO BE A MAN —
NEVER WANTING TO BE A HERO —
THIS TESTOSTERONE BEAST WHO'S ONLY
DUTY IS TO DRINK LIQUID POISON AND
DISCIPLINE — IRON FIST —
SEALING EVERY BOY'S EMOTIONS
WITH A COLDNESS WORSE THAN ANY NIGHT IN
ANTARCTICA.

NO MATTER WHERE, THE BIRDS STILL SING THE SAME

HEIGHTS OF LIFE IN THESE TREES
THAT LIVED LONGER THAN WE EVER WILL —
FROM A DISTANCE YOU ARE BUT A DOT —
THE WAY THE BIRD PREYS —
THE EYE TRAVELS AND SEES ALL —
NATURE IS THE SAME NO MATTER THE SHELL —
OIL SLICK OPERA —
YOUR MORNING SONG OF HUNGER —
THIS BREAD NEVER FILLS THE VOID —
THIS PAPER NEVER WORTH THE WASTED TIME —
SLIP THROUGH MY HANDS WITH
MORNING SHADOWS CASTING —
SIDE EYE VIEW —
FROM HERE IT IS THE SAME.

THE TORNADO AND THE SNAKE

TORNADO SMILING AS IT BRINGS THE FURY OF AGES —
THE ATROCITIES OF A HUNGRY DEMON —
THE WIND BLOWS —
IT HITS UPON US WITH SMILING CHARM —
SWIRLING LIFETIMES —
60'S CHILD BECAME 70'S WHORE —
A VAGINA SWOLLEN WITH FLUIDS OF
GENERATIONS OF LOVE —
THE WHITE WOMAN'S BASIC DEAD FLOWER —
SHE IS STRIPPED OF CULTURE LIKE
A BLANK PIECE OF PAPER THAT NEVER SEEN
A WRITTEN WORD.
FROM FAR AWAY EVERYTHING LOOKS SO APPEALING...
UNTIL IT IS BED WITH YOU.

OLD SOUL

COMMON SOUL —
COMFORT IN FEAR —
AGING LOVE —
ROLES REVERSED —
CUT THE EDGES —
DIVIDED LIKE TWO HALFS ON
EACH SIDE OF THIS DULL SWORD —
DRIED BLOOD LIKE STAINED SHEETS —
ALL THAT IS LEFT OF YOU —
GENTLE KISS —
COLD HAND —
YOUR MEMORY SEEMS SO DIFFERENT
FROM HOW I REMEMBER YOU —
HOW MANY MORE MORNINGS
CAN THIS OLD SOUL HANDLE.

OUTLOOK FADING

YOUR POSITIVE OUTLOOK ON LIFE
AND EVERYONE AROUND YOU IS DYING.
THREE LETTERS GIVE YOU FALSE HOPE —
IMAGINARY THOUGHTS —
ANGELS AND HEATHENS —
THE STATUE ALWAYS STANDING GUARD —
KEEPING REALITY OUT —
PENETRATE FALSE IDOLS —
HOW DO YOU KNOW WHEN THEY ARE TRUE?
DADDY REACHED INSIDE —
WHY STOP NOW — WHEN MY
EYE IS ALREADY BLACKENED.

PAPER MISERY

FUNNY YOU SHOULD BELIEVE IN
IMAGINARY THINGS WHEN PAPER
IS THE DRIVING FORCE FOR LIFE —
GOD OR DEVIL —
YOU CAN HOLD IT IN YOUR HAND AND IT TEARS EASY —
LIKE YOUR HAPPINESS —
THIEF OF TIME —
NEVER COMING BACK —
LIKE THE LOVE OF A PARENT YOU NEVER HAD —
LIKE A CANCER BREWING INSIDE —
PONDERANCE —
SLAVE IN THIS DUNGEON YOU CALL LIFE —
CUT OFF LIMB BY LIMB —
DOLLAR BY DOLLAR —
UNTIL THERE IS NOTHING LEFT OF US

PAPER WHORE

BLOODY KNEES —
LIFELESS RAGDOLL —
FOLLOWING THE CHAIN OF LIFE —
SLAVE TO EARTH'S DARKNESS —
THE CRACK TOO SMALL TO SLITHER
INTO THE BRIGHT LIGHT —
KISS OF BLOOD —
STAIN THE SKIN CELL —
ERECTED —
I CANNOT SEE THROUGH YOUR MOUNTAIN —
IF YOUR RESISTANCE WAS WEAK —
WOULD YOU TAKE ME TO THE
DARK PARTS OF YOUR HEART —
LIFE WHORE —
STANDING ON THE CORNERS OF YOUR MIND —
DO NOT STOP TO PICK ME UP.

PERSONALITY DISTORTION

3 FACE — 2 FACE
WHOLE BODY — SMALL IDEAS
SPLIT IN SO MANY WAYS —
WE LOOKED IN DIFFERENT DIRECTIONS —
WE WERE LOOKING FOR THE SAME THING —
THE SAME THING — DIFFERENT WAYS —
THESE PARTS UNKNOWN —
PART EMPTY.
PERSONALITY DISTORTION — 3 SAD FACES.
HE LOOKED UP — THEY LOOKED DOWN —
DO WE SHARE THE SAME MIND?
WHAT A SHAME WE CANNOT LEAVE THIS
PRISON WE CALL THE BODY.
SHADOW CORPSE —
WHERE IT ONCE HELD HOPE —
THIS BODY IS NOW BARREN.
OPEN LIKE THE EMPTY PARKING LOTS
OF THE WORLD.

PLAYING THE UNIVERSE

MOTHER OF ALL —
IT IS YOUR GENTLE VAGINA THEY FEAR —
GENTLY STRUMMING THE WORLD'S BALANCE —
A CONSTANT NOTE PLAYED IN THE KEY OF SADNESS
YOU NEVER KNOW HOW SACRED SOME THINGS ARE —
UNTIL YOU GO TO BUY IT AND IT IS NOT THERE —
THESE THINGS NO MAN CAN DESIGN OR REPLACE —
YOUR VEINS OF THE UNIVERSE —
CLOGGED WITH THE FAT OF HUMANITY —
YOU ARE MY HUMAN LANDFILL —
I DISPOSED ALL THE LOVE AND ROMANCE
I TRIED BUT THEY NEVER TRY —
SHE'S LOOKING DOWN ON YOU —
A SMIRK SAYING —
IF YOU ONLY KNEW HOW QUICKLY
I COULD CHANGE THE COURSE —
AND LEAVE YOU WANTING MORE.

PROMISE

I NEED YOU SO MUCH MORE THAN YOU NEED ME —
A WORD WEIGHED ONLY BY THE BEHOLDER —
IMPORTANCE AND VALUE THAT WOULD
BANKRUPT ANYONE —
PROMISE I HAVE HEARD YOU SO MUCH —
LIKE A RECORD THAT HAS BEEN SKIPPING —
SINCE THAT DAY IN 1997.

RETURNING TO THE DREAM

WAKE UP —
TO RETURN TO PEACE —
SOLITUDE —
MY LIVING DEAD STATE —
GIANT CIRCLE OF SOCIETY
STAYING IN YOUR LANES AND
ASSIGNED PARKING SPOTS AND
CHECK OUT LINES —
SYSTEMATIC LIKE LINED UP CATTLE-
DRAWN TO THE TV-
BRING ME BACK TO THE
DREAM STATE NIGHTLY-
SCHEDULES-
NUMBERS AND IMAGINARY
DIGITAL MONEY ARE YOUR LIFE FORCE-
NO AMBULANCE COULD ARRIVE
IN TIME TO REVIVE ME.

ROLLING TIME

ROLLING STARS —
WE GREW WITH TIME —
DID WE KNOW —
NEVER —
WE CAN SAY NOW —
STOP TO HEAR THAT WE ARE
STILL BREATHING —
FLESH 37 —
RUST —
DID YOU EVER LOSE YOUR
TRUE COLORS —
CAN WE REMEMBER —
I SEEN YOUR FLATLANDS —
THAT IS YOUR HEART —
TREE ALONE —
AFTER ALL IT WAS ME WHO NOTICED —
KEEP THESE VOICES ON MUTE —
THIS LOUDNESS —
SO DEAFENING —
WERE YOU LISTENING?

SAD DISTANCES

THE CORNERS WHERE WE GO TO FEEL NORMAL
WATCHING DANCERS GO BY —
THEY NEVER LOOKED UP TO SEE
THE BLOOD TEARS SWELLING UP IN OUR EYES —
BLACK AND RED —
AGAINST YOUR PALE BODY
DID YOU KNOW THE STAIN MY BLOOD WOULD LEAVE?
A PORTRAIT HANGING IN THE MANSION OF YOUR
HUNDRED YEAR OLD MIND
WITH A SHELL SO THICK —
TO BLOCK ALL ATTEMPTS AT INTRUSION
THERE WE WERE STANDING —
IN THE BALLROOM OF MEMORIES
I DANCED ALONE AND MOVED WITH YOUR SHADOW —
SUDDEN SHOCK —
WHEN YOU ACTUALLY TURNED TOO FAST —
AND WE BOTH WOKE UP.

SEPARATION

MY BEST FRIEND ANXIETY —
NOW MY WORST ENEMY —
I GROW WITH YOU LIKE A PRISONER
GROWS TO LOVE HIS CELL —
IS HELL ON YOUR GPS —
SOMETIMES GOOD —
HELL IS HERE —
YOU CAME TO ME SO INNOCENT
LIKE THE FIRST DAY OF KINDERGARTEN
WHEN YOUR MOTHER LEFT YOU BEHIND.
THIS IS JUST THE BEGINNING AND NOW
WE ARE 38 YEARS ON —
I HAVE GROWN TO HATE YOU.
AT TIMES ESSENTIAL —
MOST DETRIMENTAL.

SEXUAL DISORIENTATION

OPEN —
FLAMING MILLENNIAL MALE —
BRO — MANCE —
NEW IDEAS —
WE WISHED FOR THIS —
IT IS HERE —
IT IS NOT WHAT I WANTED —
GENDER SPINNING —
GENITAL MUTILATION —
NO SYMBOL —
DOORS WITH NO SIGNS —
HUMANS WITH NO IDENTITIES —
IHOMO'S IN A TECH WORLD —
VOID OF FEELING —
HETERO COCK —
HOMO COCK
TRANNY COCK —
THE POWER SYMBOL —
WE PUNCHED MOTHERS VAGINA —
THE ROOM IS SPINNING —
AS I FALL OUT OF YOUR
21ST CENTURY WOMB.

SHADOW FACE

ALWAYS THERE —
HALF A FACE —
IN THE CORNER —
HALF THE LIGHT —
CONSTANT —
LIKE AN OCEAN PULLS IT'S RIVERS —
YOU PULL TEARS —
ANY ROOM CAN SHRINK WHEN YOU
INVADE THE CORRIDORS OF MY MIND —
YOU FIND ME EVEN WHEN
I WANT TO BE LOST —
THE BEAST —
CALL IT WHATEVER SUITS YOU —
LOOKED UP —
THERE ARE ONLY 2 OF US AT
THE BACK OF THIS ROOM —
I GUESS WE WERE STUCK ON PAUSE —
WHILE THE REST ON PLAY.

SILENCE THE STARS

DARK SKY WITH NO ONE BUT LIGHT YEARS —
FOR A COMPANION —
DEAFENING SILENCE —
IN THE DISCO AFTERLIFE —
LIBERACE THE TOUR GUIDE —
IN OUR T-CELL PROM —
YOU CAME ALONE —
WITH CRYPTIC SOUND OF SILENCE —
PUNCH THROUGH THE HEARTLAND —
DADDY IN WRANGLERS —
I STARED FROM THE WINDOW —
IMAGINING MY GREAT ESCAPE —
GENERATION POISON —
I KISSED YOUR MOUTH TO STOP THE BLEEDING —
NO WORDS SPOKEN —
THE SILENCE OUR UNSPOKEN BOND —
THE DISEASE WAR THAT NO ONE WINS.

SKYWARD INNOCENCE

BENDING — SKYWARD —
FOLLOWING SPIRIT —
TRAPPED INNOCENCE —
PROTECTION —
RADIATING THOUGHT.
MIND ON FIRE —
EYES CLOSED —
EYES BARELY OPEN — NO EYES SEEING.
RAW AND YET DIVINE.
THE BUSH OF THE BODY —
THE BUSH YOU HIDE IN.
THIS PROTECTION — IT WEEPS —
WE BOTH WEEPED — NOTHING THERE TO DRY THE EYE.
2 GENDER — LIMITLESS SEXUAL ORGAN —
THE BRAIN —
SO LITTLE BUT ONE DAY THE ORGAN WILL GROW —
THE PHYSICAL NEVER MATCHING THE UNSEEN.
SMALL MIND — BIG IDEAS —
THE MOTHER REALLY KNOWS WHAT THE CHILD HIDES.

SPARK

ONE DAY I LOOKED AWAY FROM THE
IDIOT BOX AND FOR THE FIRST TIME I REALLY SEEN —
THE CLOUDS —
DID YOU STARE TO THE BOTTOM OF THE
GLASS — WHICH WAS ALWAYS HALF EMPTY —
MAYBE EVERY ROAD MUST END —
EVERY STRAIGHT LINE MUST TURN —
CURVES —
SO MANY —
THOSE SHOES YOU WALKED IN SO MUCH —
NOTHING LEFT —
YOU KNOW THIS ROUTE TOO WELL —
TRY WALKING PATHS UNKNOWN —
SPARK.

SPIRIT DANCING — BODY IDLE

WALL LEANING — CORPSE STILL
INTERNAL FEEL — OUTER ISOLATION.
YOUR MOVEMENT — OBSCENELY EROTIC —
OUTSIDE SHELL.
A GLIMPSE INSIDE
DO I HAVE TO FIGHT AND
CRAWL TO GET INSIDE YOU?
DO NOT BE SO ATTAINABLE
THE MYSTERY AND LURE DRAWS ME IN
YOU COULDN'T TELL —
LIVING IN YOUR OWN HEAD.
SOMBER — HEAD DOWN —
INSIDE SWIRLING MOVEMENT
RADIATING
BUT ONLY FOR CERTAIN EYES
THAT PIERCE DARK
SHADOWS.
IN YOUR WORLD WHERE
THERE IS NO ONE BUT YOU
AM I INVITED?

STACKED SOULS

ALL THE SPIRITS THAT CROSSED
INTO MY LANE OF LIFE —
SO MANY STACKED SOULS —
SO MUCH WASTED PASSION —
SO MUCH STOLEN TIME —
ALL THOSE INHALED BREATHS THAT
I FOOLISHLY THOUGHT WERE GIVING ME LIFE —
WERE SLOWLY KILLING ME —
I GUESS FOREVER WAS 36 MONTHS
IN A SLUTS WORLD —
WE DO NOT USE CALENDARS —
WE DO NOT USE CLOCKS —
BECAUSE TIME IS NOT VALUABLE HERE.

STIFLED GROWTH

SCREAMING FIERCELY —
IN STOP MOTION — FROZEN —
THE LOUDEST SOUND.
STAY WHERE YOU ARE —
IT IS THERE THAT YOU FEEL COMFORT —
BUT IS IT DISGUISED —
AWAITING — BARE
IN THE TRACKS OF A CIRCLE YOU THOUGHT
WAS TAKING YOU SOMEWHERE.
WHEN YOU LOOK DOWN AT THE LINES
OF THIS HIGHWAY WITH NO MARKERS —
WOULD YOU KNOW THE DIFFERENCE IN 100 MILES?
LOOK BACK —
LOOK FORWARD —
DO YOU SEE THE DIFFERENCE?
THERE IS NONE.
IN YOUR EYES I SCREAMED WITH NO SOUND —
YOU CHOSE TO IGNORE THE MOUTH
SO WIDE IN LIFE'S MIRROR.

SYSTEMATIC CLOSET

RED ROSE FETUS —
BIRTHED BY THE SEED OF A CONFUSED MAN
WE MAKE LOVE 10 MINS HERE AND THERE IN SECRET —
ELUSIVE TO BABY — DID HE KNOW DADDY
WAS ALWAYS WANTING TO KNOW
WHAT IT FELT LIKE TO BE MOMMY?
GENDER ROLES REVERSED THIS TIME
LAYING ON YOUR BACK LOOKING UP AT THE SKY —
TROLLING THROUGH THE
SEEDY PARTS OF HUMAN SEXUALITY
THE GHETTO OF THE MIND —
THE GUTTER WHERE WE LIVE IN MINUTE INTERVALS —
SKELETAL REAPER —
WE TAKE THIS SECRET TO DEATH —
HE WAITS —
THE JOURNEY OF THE MAN WITH THE COVERED FACE —
THE SHAME YOU WALKED PAST
BUT WHEN WE LAY NAKED
IT IS THERE YOU FEEL A PART OF YOUR TRUTH —
BUT ONLY FOR MINUTES AT A TIME.

TEN PERCENT UNKNOWING

MYSTERY SCREEN —
YOUR WARRIOR BEHIND
THE PLASTIC ALPHABET —
SHADOW OF COMFORT —
NOW THE SHADOW AT THE END OF
THIS UNIVERSAL BED WITH KNIFE —
ADJUST YOUR EYES SIR —
THIS IS A 3AM REALITY —
THE RED SUN AND RED STAR —
SQUINTING EYES SEE NO TRUTHS
WHEN BLINDFOLDED BY LOVE —
SPEEDING TO NEVER —
CUT THE EYES OUT BUT LEAVE
THE MIND TO QUESTION —
HOW THIS COULD BE —
STRANGER IN THE BLACK ALLEY
WITH A BREATHLESS KISS.

THE EYE OF WHIRLING EMOTION

STUCK IN A FURY OF CHAOS —
LIKE AN ISLAND —
CENTERED TURMOIL THAT
CANNOT BE ESCAPED —
BECAUSE TO TRY TO SWIM AWAY
WOULD SURELY MEAN MY DEATH
BUT TO STAY ON THIS ISLAND —
IS THE SAME AS DYING INSIDE
CENTERED AMONGST FURY —
FURY IN ME-BLACK LINE —
IT'S THE DEADLINE —
BLOOD PUMPING SWIRLS —
IF SO MUCH RECYCLED BLOOD IS INSIDE —
THEN WHY IS MY HEART NOT BEATING.

THE ONLY DIFFERENCE BETWEEN ME AND THE PAVEMENT IS I FEEL

GREY AND BLANK FOR MILES —
IF I LAID MY PAIN OUT WOULD IT
EQUAL THE DISTANCE BETWEEN —
HEART TIRED —
LIMBS ACHE —
DOES THE PAVEMENT FEEL LIKE
THESE BLACK ORGANS —
SILENT VOICES IN THE HEADS OF FEW —
HEARING AND LISTENING —
DO YOU KNOW THE DIFFERENCE —
CRACKS FOR MILES —
THE COURSE OF THESE VEINS —
A VESSEL FOR LIFE'S FLUID —
THE COLOR OF CONFUSION —
FROZEN AND NUMB.

THE PAST IS UNFIXABLE

ERRORS IN REVERSE —
REFLECT ENERGY USELESS —
I CRAVE THE ROAD THAT IS NOW
NOTHING BUT TREES —
THE MYSTERY IS IN THERE STILL —
I CANNOT SEE —
THOUGHTS COVERED MY EYES OR
WAS IT YOUR MEMORY SMOTHERING ME —
CHOKING THE PAST THAT NEVER DIED —
GASPING —
THE ASSEMBLY LINE OF LIFE —
ONE OF A KIND —
DNA —
FINGERPRINT —
THESE THINGS THAT REQUIRE MORE
THAN GLUE TO STAY TOGETHER —
WHEN YOU SWALLOW IT ALL AND ALL
THAT IS LEFT IS THE FAINT SCENT OF A MAN.

THE PEDAL DETERMINES

THE FORCE OF MY WILL
THE PRESSURE OF MY DESIRE —
DETERMINES IF YOU LIVE —
OR YOUR SPIRIT DIES
WILL THE CHEMICALS OF
MY MIND CRASH INTO YOU
REASONING UNDETERMINED IN A RUSH —
SECONDS DETERMINED YEARS
THE ECHO BEHIND YOUR WORDS —
THE EMPTY SPACES —
AFTER ALL AREN'T ALL WORDS EMPTY —
FILL IN BLANK INTENTIONS
YOU FELL INTO THE HOLE
BECAUSE TRUST WAS NOT
STRONG ENOUGH TO HOLD YOU UP
EVERY CHANCE IS A RISK —
THE RISK TOO MUCH
THE DEBT OF YOUR HEART
COULD NEVER BE PAID BACK —
BANKRUPT ROMANCE.

THE SIZE OF SMALL

YOU LAID ON A BARREN GROUND —
IN THIS URBAN CHAOS —
LITTLE HEART THAT WAS
ONCE BEATING SO FAST —
IS NOW SLOWLY FADING —
INCONSEQUENTIAL TO MOST —
COULD YOU SEE ME FROM THE TOP —
OF THE TALLEST BUILDING?
THE WAY I LOOKED UP —
FROM THE GROUND AND SEEN YOU —
BARRIERS —
ALWAYS A BARRIER —
A BLOCK —
A REASON NOT TO CARE —
BUT I LOOKED DOWN AND FELT SORROW —
WHERE MANY WOULD NOT HAVE VENTURED —
SNAPSHOT OF A FADING SPIRIT —
DID I CAPTURE YOUR SOUL IN OUR PASSING?
DID YOU CURSE THIS HUMAN WORLD
WITH YOUR LAST BREATH?
YOU MEANT SOMETHING TO ME.

THE SOIL CYCLES

RETURN TO ME SAID THE GROUND —
DID YOU STARE LONG ENOUGH
TO SEE THE CALLING —
LIFE CYCLE —
HALF SKELETAL —
HALF FLESH —
THE SIDE ROAD OF LIFE —
LEFT TO DECOMPOSE —
NO ONE'S MEMORY —
WE STARTED HERE AND WE END HERE —
THIS BRICK SLAVE SYSTEM YOU BUILT
YOURSELF MEANS NOTHING IN THE END —
THE LIFE RECEIPT —
THE PAPER MILE MARKERS —
SUN GROWN HUMAN —
MELT BACK INTO EARTH —
THE SOIL ALWAYS CALLS US BACK —
DID YOU SPEND YOUR LIFE LISTENING
OR DID THE SCREAMING LIFE DEAFEN YOU?

THE TORNADO AND THE SNAKE

TORNADO SMILING AS IT BRINGS THE FURY OF AGES —
THE ATROCITIES OF A HUNGRY DEMON —
THE WIND BLOWS —
IT HITS UPON US WITH SMILING CHARM —
SWIRLING LIFETIMES —
60'S CHILD BECAME 70'S WHORE —
A VAGINA SWOLLEN WITH FLUIDS OF
GENERATIONS OF LOVE —
THE WHITE WOMAN'S BASIC DEAD FLOWER —
SHE IS STRIPPED OF CULTURE LIKE
A BLANK PIECE OF PAPER THAT NEVER SEEN
A WRITTEN WORD.
FROM FAR AWAY EVERYTHING LOOKS SO APPEALING...
UNTIL IT IS IN BED WITH YOU

THOUGHT SEEPER

YOU INVADER —
YOU THIEF —
YOU HOLD MY MIND HOSATGE —
THOUGHT SEEPER —
OUT OF NOWHERE —
YOU SHOW YOURSELF IN MY MIND —
SOMEWHERE YOU LIVE AND
HAVE RENT FREE FOR YEARS —
NO COST COULD EVER ADD UP TO COMPENSATE —
FOR ALL YOU HAVE TAKEN FROM ME IN SPIRIT —
THE EYE THAT LAYS SILENT —
BUT SEES THE UGLY WORLD —
THROUGH IT'S LAST REMAINING GAZE —
ATTENTION DEFICIT HEART —
YOU JUMP AROUND SO MUCH —
BUT NEVER STAY ON THAT
TINY MENTAL ISLAND CALLED PEACE —
FOR VERY LONG —
DO YOU HAVE AN OFF SWITCH?

TIRED BRUISED BRAIN

FULL OF HEAVY MEMORIES —
SO MANY THAT YOU BURNT OUT LIKE AN
EXTERNAL HARD DRIVE OF THE MIND —
A FUNNY THING YOU BLOCK —
JUST TO KEEP YOURSELF ALIVE —
A SHIELD OF PAIN —
LAYERS DEEP —
VAST HEARTACHE —
NUMB —
I SEE AND HEAR BUT —
I CANNOT ABSORB —
I REFLECT BACK — IF ONLY MY SUN
WAS HAPPY AND SHINING —
LIKE YOURS —
WE SEE THINGS DIFFERENTLY —
YOU KNOW.

TORMENTED BLISS

SCRATCHING AT THE WALLS OF A TORMENTED MIND —
MOMENTS OF BLISS —
HEARING NOISES —
PARANOIA PREVAILS —
FIST PUNCHING THROUGH THE UTERUS OF SUBURBIA —
CAGES WE DESIGNED WITH LITTLE PLASTIC CARDS —
3AM PEACE —
WE MOVED UP FROM THE BACK OF THE ROOM —
THE NORMAL —
YOUR COLOR SELDOM USED WAS THE BRIGHTEST —
THE CRACK IN THE PRESCRIPTION BOTTLE
WAS HOW THE LIGHT GOT IN.

TOUGH BOY WITH THE PAINTED LIPS

PUSSY BOY —
SMEARED SELF ESTEEM —
X WRITTEN ON THE MIRROR —
DID YOU SEE YOUR TRUE SELF THERE —
MUSCLE OF WEAK HEARTS —
SLIPPED THROUGH THE MUSTACHE MAN —
DOMINANCE —
YOU RODE IN ON 1000 HORSES —
CIGARETTE DANGLING —
SPIT ON ME IF YOU LOVE ME —
LAYING SO VULNERABLE —
WE DO NOT SPEAK OF FOREVER —
WE SPEAK OF THIS RUSHED MOMENT —
YOUR STAMP ON ME IS WEARING OFF —
AS YOUR "WIFE" WHISPERED IN MY EAR.

UNDERSTANDING

FROZEN — COLD — MATERIAL WORLD
LIKE MUSIC YOU START AND STOP WHEN
I NEED YOU MOST.
I SMOTHER YOU LIKE
RAIN SMOTHERS THE RIVER — OVERFLOWING —
COME BACK TO ME LIKE THE CIRCLE OF LIFE —
EACH TIME YOU PASS THROUGH ME —
I GET WEAKER —
IMAGINARY EMBRACE LIKE
A THOUSAND BEAMS HOLDING UP
THE TALLEST BUILDINGS OF MY DREAMS —
KEEP GOING UNTIL WE GET TO THE TOP —
YOU TOLD ME WE COULD FLY —
BUT I JUMPED ALONE.

WALKING MILES WITH THE BIBLE ON YOUR BACK

INNOCENCE ILLUSIONS —
HONESTY —
LOYALTY —
EMOTIONALLY DEAD —
LIAR —
A CAREER OF HIDING —
PROFESIONAL BULSHIT —
SCARS LEFT NEVER HEALING —
MAKE UP —
MANY TIMES —
LAYERS —
ABANDONMENT —
NEVER THERE —
LONLEY/ALONE —
WITH YOU NEXT TO ME —
MOTHER/FATHER —
BROTHER —
ROOTS —
RUNNING DETACHED —
SEVERITY —
FACE IT QUICK —
IT IS COMING AT 100MPH —
THE BRICK WALL —
ITS BLACK NOW.

YOU CAN ONLY GO BACK IN YOUR HEAD

CAN YOU GO BACKWARDS ON THIS ROAD —
ASKED THE PASSENGER —
IMAGINE THESE THINGS —
THE SUN BLOCKED MEMORIES —
FADED AMBITIONS —
A BRAIN STUCK ON REWIND —
FIGHTING A FOOT MOVING FORWARD —
FALLING IN LIFE'S POTHOLES —
A RIVER IN REVERSE —
DROWNING IN IMAGINARY OCEANS —
IN MY MIND I SLOWLY FLOATED TO THE BOTTOM —
YOU CAN ONLY GO BACK IN YOUR HEAD.

CONTACT ME ON TWITTER @JASONCONEAL
https://twitter.com/JASONCONEAL

CONTACT ME ON FACEBOOK AT:
https://www.facebook.com/SHADOWSWITHNOLIGHT

FOLLOW ME ON INSTAGRAM AT:
https://www.instagram.com/jason_c_oneal

EMAIL ME AT: SHADOWSWITHNOLIGHT@GMAIL.COM

www.ingramcontent.com/pod-product-compliance
Lightning Source LLC
Chambersburg PA
CBHW020659300426
44112CB00007B/449